WORLD ECONOMY EXPLAINED

International Trade

VV
FRANKLIN WATTS
LONDON•SYDNEY

 An Appleseed Editions book

First published in 2010 by Franklin Watts
338 Euston Road, London NW1 3BH

Franklin Watts Australia
Hachette Children's Books
Level 17/207 Kent St, Sydney, NSW 2000

© 2010 Appleseed Editions

Created by Appleseed Editions Ltd,
Well House, Friars Hill, Guestling,
East Sussex TN35 4ET

Designed by Helen James
Edited by Mary-Jane Wilkins
Picture research by Su Alexander

ISBN 978 1 4451 0043 2

Dewey Classification: 382

A CIP catalogue for this book is available from the British Library.

Photograph acknowledgements
page 6 Photofusion Picture Library/Alamy; 9 Roger Ressmeyer/Corbis; 10 North Wind
Picture Archives/Alamy; 13 Roger Wood/Corbis; 14 Haruyoshi Yamaguchi/Corbis;
15 David Bergman/Corbis; 19 James L Amos/Corbis; 20 Syed Jan Sabawoon/epa/Corbis;
22 Jehad Nga/Corbis; 25 Ed Wolfstein/epa/Corbis; 26 Andrew Holbrooke/Corbis; 29
Todd Reese/Alamy; 30 Jon Arnold Images Ltd/Alamy; 32 Worldwide Picture Library/
Alamy; 34 Yoan Valat/epa/Corbis; 36 James Leynse/Corbis; 38 Chris McLennan/
Alamy; 40 Andy Rain/epa/Corbis; 42 Daniel Deme/epa/Corbis
Front cover UrbanLandscapes/Alamy

Printed in China

Franklin Watts is a division of Hachette Children's Books,
an Hachette UK company.
www.hachette.co.uk

Contents

It's a small world

Most of us think of our everyday lives as locally based, as we go to school or work and then later relax at home or out with friends. Few of us imagine that in the course of an ordinary day we are connected at many levels with international trade. Yet all our lives are based on international connections, from the moment we take our first bite of breakfast until we settle under the bedclothes at night.

The goods we buy and consume are made all over the world, and our lives would be much less interesting if we could not get hold of them. British families buy Japanese cars, watch American films and eat butter that has crossed half the globe from New Zealand. Americans download British music, buy Italian clothing and drink Brazilian coffee.

Meanwhile, some countries that once supplied goods to richer countries are now wealthy enough to import goods from other parts of the world. The two countries with the largest populations in the world, China and India, now have fast-growing economies. Their people are developing tastes for foreign goods to match those of Americans, Europeans or Australians.

Exchange and fairness

Any exchange of goods and services can be described as trade. Trading is a natural human instinct. Without any prompting from adults, children trade football cards, stamps and conkers. Sometimes money changes hands, and sometimes the trade is just that – a swap.

Opposite: children swap trading cards in a northern English suburb; many people have first-hand experience of trading which goes back to childhood.

In many ways international trade is just a much larger version of those playground trades. People from one country decide that something produced in another country will sell well at home. So a British company might set up an office in Thailand to buy Thai prawn crackers and send them to Britain for sale. People in Thailand might be eager to buy Manchester United football kits or music by Lily Allen. All these sales are international trade.

Just as an angry child might cry 'not fair' if his friend suggests a one-sided conker trade, countries can also be dissatisfied with their international trade. For many years, wealthier developed countries set the terms for international trade. Initially they did this by using – or threatening to use – their military strength. In that way, they forced weaker countries to trade their goods, and not always on terms that were fair. Some people argue that the same countries still have the upper hand in the area of international trade, but now their power comes through the strength of their companies.

International organizations (see pages 34-37) now try to keep a balance between achieving the best trading deals for every country and ensuring that all sides agree that those deals are fair. This balancing act is one of the major challenges of the twenty-first century.

Trade: ancient and modern

The earliest human societies valued trading highly. Many experts believe that trade was a driving force in helping primitive societies develop into more advanced civilizations. The earliest groupings of humans were family groups living in basic conditions – for example, in the shelter of a cave – and struggling every day to find food and keep themselves clothed. These hunter-gatherer communities had little time to make goods to trade with other groups. Every day was a struggle for survival.

This first period of human society is called the Stone Age because people shaped stone into tools and weapons. Some stones, such as flint, can be formed more easily into sharp weapons than others. Bits of flint and other useful stones have been found among the bones of Stone Age people far from any natural source of flint. Experts believe that early humans traded these useful stones for food or fur.

Cultivating trade

From about 10,000 years ago, people found ways to cultivate food plants rather than spend time and effort looking for them. Staying in one place, with a regular food supply, allowed people to build permanent settlements. These early societies found grains to suit their climate and landscape, beginning with wheat and barley in the Middle East. Around 5000 years ago, people in what is now China had begun to grow rice, and native Americans in Mexico had learned to plant and harvest maize and beans.

Having learned to grow crops to satisfy their basic needs, people then turned to cultivating less essential crops. Grapes and olives – grown to be turned into wine and oil – were first cultivated in western Asia, but by 3500 BC they had become common crops in Greece and the eastern Mediterranean.

About the same time the ancient Egyptians and Sumerians established trading routes to exchange precious metals and jewels. They also developed written communication to a high level, and their extensive records tell us about how trade grew. Even more detailed records chart the growth of trade in ancient Greece and Rome.

By about 200 BC, this established trading network in southern Europe and western Asia began to forge links with the trading power that had developed in East Asia – China. The Silk Route (see pages 12-13) began the development of global trade, with goods travelling east and west 10,000 km or further.

The modern era

Many trading links survived the fall of the Roman Empire in the fifth century AD. New countries such as France and England developed in Europe, trading with each other and with regions beyond Europe.

Craftsmen transported massive stones over great distances to build Stonehenge more than 4000 years ago – they are evidence of ancient trading routes.

Even the Vikings, who attacked much of Europe in the ninth and tenth centuries, helped spread trade. Ireland's capital city, Dublin, was founded as a Viking trading post.

In the fifteenth century, European explorers began to find new sea routes to link up with trading partners in Asia. They followed the coast of Africa south and then east to reach the Indian Ocean.

When Christopher Columbus set out in 1492, he was looking for a short cut to Asia when he reached America. In the event, his discovery provided Spain and other European powers with a vast new trading area. The colonies that European powers set up in the Americas, Asia and Africa were all based on trade.

Native Americans board a French ship to trade animal furs in the early 1600s. Many Europeans made fortunes from their trade links with the New World.

Personal account

EASY EXCHANGES

Captain Arthur Barlowe led an English expedition in 1584 to raid land that the Spanish had claimed in North America. In this account, he describes meeting a group of native Americans in what is now North Carolina. The local people were eager to trade deer skins for the metal objects that the Englishmen carried with them.

Barlowe's description suggests that this trading was carried out in a friendly, trusting fashion – unlike most other exchanges between Europeans and Native Americans: 'We exchanged our tinne dish for twentie skinnes, woorth twentie Crownes [£5]… and a copper kettle for fiftie skinnes woorth fifty Crownes [£12.50]. They offered us good exchange for our hatchets, and axes, and for knives, and would have given any thing for swordes: but wee would not depart with any.'

The global dimension

International trade has continued to drive societies, and our modern world has come to depend on trade more and more. This dependence can have drawbacks – buying and selling goods around the world also means that economic troubles can spread quickly via the same routes.

The leaders of the 20 richest countries in the world met in London in April 2009 to find a way of coping with the international economic crisis known as the credit crunch. Each of those countries – as well as dozens of poorer countries – had been suffering the effects of economic problems since 2007. But no single country can dig itself out of trouble without the cooperation of other countries.

To make things more complicated, some voters believed that the actions of their leaders created the recent problems, rather than intertwined actions worldwide. Those leaders need to convince voters that a long-term solution must be international.

Building up world trade

According to the World Trade Organization, in 2008 international trade was worth about £11 trillion. That figure was about 50 times greater than the 1970 amount, and provides evidence of how quickly international trade has grown. The jump also shows how scientific and technological innovations can have a dramatic effect on the way countries trade with one another.

The rocketing increase in trade coincided with equally rapid advances in computer technology, especially the development of the Internet. People have always been quick to turn almost every scientific or technological advance into a money-making venture. The history of world trade is proof of that aspect of human nature.

Continuing trends

The huge trading centres of Europe and the Middle East on one hand, and of China on the other, had been separate for many hundreds of years. During that time, both sides had goods the other desired. Europe and western Asia had gold, while China had luxuries such as silk. The main obstacles, apart from deserts and mountains, were thieves. Once the armies of the Roman empire offered support to merchants, caravans could make the long journey to link Europe with Asia.

In the age before paved roads, sea travel could offer a much quicker way of travelling long distances. Boat-builders in Europe and Asia designed sailing ships which cut this travelling time. The time they saved could mean arriving at a port before a competitor's ships – and making a fortune in trade before they arrived. Faster sailing ships such as clippers were eventually replaced by steamships and other powered craft,

Instant trading

The late twentieth century brought an age of instant communications. People's lives were changed through radio and television, which allowed them to hear and see world events unfold as they happened. The rapid development of computers was another feature of this new age, and it continues to offer new ways of sending information back and forth in an instant. Instant communication – using whichever medium – has revolutionized the way we conduct international trade. Individuals and companies can scan the globe for the best products, check prices, place orders and pay for goods in a matter of seconds. And in the case of products such as computer software, their purchases can be sent along the same lines of communication. All this would have been hard to imagine – let alone explain – 50 years ago.

while at the same time railways began to link countries and even continents. When cars and trucks – and eventually aircraft – arrived on the scene at the beginning of the twentieth century, the stage was set for faster trading in much greater quantities.

A series of inns, called caravanserais, provided comfortable stops for traders along the Silk Route. This caravanserai is at the edge of the Great Salt Desert in central Iran.

How economies work

We can study international trade at the highest level and make detailed predictions using the latest computer technology. National leaders take advice from teams of economists who use those methods. Together they aim to increase trade in ways that promote national interests and can continue into the future.

Opposite: eager fans wait for the arrival of Harry Potter *star Daniel Radcliffe before a film opening in Tokyo. Films and other cultural exports boost the economies of the countries in which they are made.*

The world of international trade is complicated, and it might take years to understand every aspect of how the world economy operates. Even experts often disagree on what to do next. Ordinary people are often the final judges of how well expert advice works in the real world: some governments have been voted out of power because of the way they are seen to have handled their country's economy. But at a simple level, international trade can still be compared with schoolchildren trading conkers or Stone Age communities trading stone tools for fur.

Basic similarities

At the most basic level, countries (or more exactly, the companies in these countries) try to trade so they have the best advantage. They export goods and services which are either abundant (for example the oil in many Middle Eastern countries) or

Some bands such as Coldplay (seen here on US television) are internationally recognized 'brands' just as Coca-Cola and Nike sports shoes are.

which they are good at supplying (for example, American films or French cheeses). In return they might import goods which cannot be grown or produced in their own countries (for example, the Swiss import cod and salmon and Britain imports tea and coffee).

Most countries allow their citizens to set up companies to export and import goods. This system is called capitalism. The companies make a profit if they are successful, and their success also benefits their country because the successful companies create jobs and pay taxes which go to the government.

Through much of the twentieth century, some countries experimented with a different type of government called communism. In communist countries, individuals could not set up their own

Personal account

EVERYDAY LIFE UNDER COMMUNISM

Although communist governments were happy to trade some products with other countries, ordinary people rarely benefited. Some factories received raw ingredients to produce street lamps, tractors, ploughs and other essential products. But shops in cities and towns had very few goods from other countries. People had little knowledge of fashion – because foreign clothes and fashion magazines were not available – and the choice of foods was very narrow.

Sonya, now in her thirties, remembers life under communism in Kursk, a large city in southern Russia: 'We could always tell foreigners by their bright clothes; our own seemed to be drab and poorly made. We never starved – in fact, we often saw photographs of poor people in America – but the food wasn't very nice. The best things like cheese and good cuts of pork were rationed. In the food shops we barely ever saw some things that are common now – oranges, bananas and coconuts, for example – because these foods came from abroad. In fact, the real treats were not for sale at all. These were the mushrooms and berries that we gathered ourselves in the woods and meadows outside the city.'

companies, and the government controlled all the jobs. This major difference meant that communist governments made all the decisions about what to import and export. Ordinary people had little or no say in these decisions, and shops usually had a poor selection of products (see Personal account).

New types of trade

For centuries, international trade involved the exchange of goods, such as raw materials, fuel, finished products, food and luxuries. These goods were traded either for other goods or for money. In the last 50 years services have come to play an important part in world trade – and they are growing in value every year. Entertainment, insurance and banking are all services because they rely on experience and skills rather than materials.

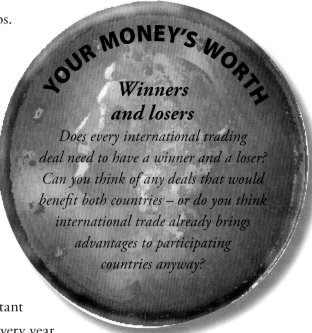

YOUR MONEY'S WORTH

Winners and losers

Does every international trading deal need to have a winner and a loser? Can you think of any deals that would benefit both countries – or do you think international trade already brings advantages to participating countries anyway?

Britain was one of the first countries to recognize the contribution that entertainment and other service industries made to the national economy. The best-selling pop group of the 1960s was the Beatles; millions of their records were sold around the world. In 1965, the four members of the group were awarded the MBE to honour their services to the export industry. More than 40 years on, British musical acts still earn vast sums abroad. In April 2009, the *New Musical Express* magazine reported that British pop musicians had earned nearly £140 million in 2008 alone – a figure that had risen by £19 million over the previous year, despite the credit crunch.

Other countries have recognized the important economic contribution made by music and other art forms. India, for example, is now the world's largest producer of films, making about a thousand every year. Many of those films have an international appeal, earning India millions in export sales.

Which system works best?

US president Calvin Coolidge, who was in power in the 1920s, was a man of few words. However, he is famous for a quote that highlights his belief in the importance of trade to his country: 'the chief business of the American people is business.'

Many political leaders might have said the same thing about their countries, but by the early twentieth century America had become the world's most powerful economy and an example for many other countries.

The conclusion that many people draw from such statements – if my country's trade is successful then other successes will follow – can lead to a number of questions. The most important is: does business success always have positive benefits for the country as a whole? Following on from that, people might also ask: does every business success help a country, or are some types of trading deals embarrassing or even harmful to their national reputation?

Profit at all costs?

One reason that communist systems (see pages 14-17) generally failed was that their export representatives had no real reason to push for success. After all, they were not able to make any money themselves, apart from their basic pay. On the other hand, people involved with private companies – the life blood of the capitalist system – can share in the success of their trading triumphs. But does that sort of success always lead to benefits for others?

If the subject is creating jobs, then the answer is 'not necessarily'. Many companies choose to get rid of highly-paid workers in their home country and move their operation to another country where pay is lower.

Many capitalist countries use lower-paid foreign workers to save money. These Turkish women are harvesting grapes in a vineyard in southern Germany.

This can save companies money, or even help them to increase their profits, but it does little to help workers at home.

Then there is the issue of companies becoming so large that they can move into another country and crush companies already there. The behaviour of these transnational companies often leads to resentment abroad, which harms the image of the companies and (sometimes) their home countries.

Personal account

POPPIES AND POVERTY

The international trade in illegal drugs such as heroin causes hardship and can even kill the people who eventually buy the drugs. But because so much money is at stake, this trade continues to grow. One of the largest suppliers of heroin is the war-torn south Asian country of Afghanistan. There the government has to fight not only the terrorist group al Qaeda and the Islamic extremist Taliban, but also the drug industry which both those groups support in order to raise money. The real losers are the Afghan farmers who grow the poppies which are processed into heroin.

Abdul Manan Farahi, head of Afghanistan's counter-terrorism police, says: 'The main point is this. The farmers are almost the victims of the dealings between al Qaeda, Taliban, and the drug mafia. The farmers in Afghanistan do not gain much from poppies and drugs except suffering because the poppies and harvest is bought very cheap.'

EXAMINATION CLOSER EXAMINATION **CLOSER EXAMINATION** CLOSER EXAMINATION CLOSER

Just your cup of tea

Hidden behind some of the most everyday products is a surprisingly complicated network of international trade. Some of the foodstuffs that we take for granted have involved labour and trade in several different countries – or even continents. A cup of tea, so typically British, is a good example.

The tea itself could come from India, China or Kenya. It might have been dried and packed using machinery from Germany. Then a Greek-owned cargo ship might transport the tea to a port in Britain. A British tea-drinker might drive her Japanese car to buy a packet of tea at the local supermarket. Back home, the tea might be made with water boiled in a stylish Italian chrome kettle and poured into delicate French teacups. Maybe the drinkers will add a spoonful of sugar from Barbados or a few drops of lemon juice from Spain.

YOUR MONEY'S WORTH

The arms trade

More than £21 billion is made every year by selling weapons. Producing and trading weapons plays an important part in many national economies. Most weapons manufacturers would argue that their products provide countries with

security and the means to defend themselves, as well as providing jobs. Do you agree, or do you believe that trading in weapons increases the likelihood of war or terrorist attacks?

Risk and disruption

Almost everyone agrees that international trade is a good thing. It ensures that people have a wide variety of things to buy while at the same time providing income for governments, companies and workers. But free trade – which is the goal for many supporters of this international economic activity – is rarely completely free. Many things can stand in its way; some are unavoidable, whereas others are deliberate obstacles.

Women prepare dinner in a camp for people made homeless by fighting in Darfur. More than two million people have lost their homes – and work – since a civil war broke out in this western region of Sudan in 2003.

The credit crunch

Since the middle of 2007, the world has been struggling through a difficult economic period called the credit crunch. The term credit gives a clue to its origins in the world of banking, but the problems soon spread to affect every part of the world economy. Most individuals and companies are constantly borrowing and repaying money from banks – to buy cars or houses, or to build up a business. This borrowing is called credit.

For some years, when house prices were rising quickly, American banks offered credit to many people who would otherwise not have been allowed to borrow money because there was a high risk that they would not be able to repay it. Banks felt that they would be able to take over their houses – and sell them at a profit – if the borrowers ran into difficulties. Many borrowers did get into financial trouble, but by early 2007 the rise in house prices had gone into reverse. Banks could take over the houses, but they found them hard to sell – and if they did sell, the price did not cover the money they were owed.

The world banking system is linked and as American banks got into trouble because of the toxic debt which resulted from irresponsible lending, banks in other countries were also drawn in. As banks found it hard to raise money, they reduced the amount they would lend (credit). The sudden withholding of credit (the crunch) affected all sorts of businesses around the world. British prime minister Gordon Brown described the process as a 'power cut'.

Companies made less money in the downturn and started to get rid of workers, which meant that more people began to feel the effects of the crunch. People had less money to spend, so international trade also suffered. By early 2009, international leaders had come up with some plans to help the world economy (see pages 42-43), but the mood remained anxious.

International trade suffers badly in countries which are going through a major crisis such as a natural disaster or war. If the disruption is serious or goes on a long time, the country's infrastructure is affected. This makes it impossible for people to trade safely and efficiently. Disruption also makes life more difficult for people in that country.

The Darfur region of Sudan has suffered civil wars and famine for 30 years. Travelling to many of the worst-affected villages in Darfur is both difficult and dangerous. Today, trade has trickled to a standstill along with many hungry people's chances of getting food and other essential supplies.

Terrorist groups often target international trade both to draw attention to themselves and to damage their target. In 2002 and 2005, an Indonesian terrorist group planted bombs on the island of Bali, killing more than 200 people (many of them foreigners). Bali is a popular tourist destination, which earns valuable income from its foreign visitors. The attacks made many foreign tourists avoid Bali, and created economic problems for the country for years.

The 9/11 terrorist attacks on New York City devastated the twin towers of the World Trade Center, which were symbols of international trade. George W. Bush, US president at the time, said that American freedom and values had been attacked. Some people saw the US-led invasion of Iraq two years later as both a response to the 9/11 attacks and a way of ensuring a continued trade in oil from that troubled region.

Many countries limit free trade either by giving special advantages to their own producers (for example, by subsidising farmers) or by imposing limits on imports in order to safeguard jobs for their own citizens. These are called protectionist measures. They are often popular at home but unpopular with trading partners. If other countries think that a protectionist action is too harsh, they may take similar action to protect their own companies when trading with the same partners.

Personal account

PIRACY OR PROTECTION?

Somalia, on the east coast of Africa, lies near some of the busiest shipping lanes in the world. Ships travelling between Europe and Asia pass through the Indian Ocean just off the country's coast. These waters are also rich in tuna, drawing in fishing fleets from around the world. Since the early 1990s, when Somalia suffered a devastating civil war, many fishing boats have taken advantage of the country's weakness and fished in Somalian waters.

Local fishermen tackled this illegal fishing by arming themselves and attacking foreign fishing boats. Soon, however, they began to go further by capturing cargo ships and demanding ransoms – usually amounting to millions of dollars. Piracy was in the headlines for the first time

in centuries as the world considered how to deal with the problem. The pirates believe they have been misunderstood and that the original problem – fishing – is still the focus. Sugule Ali, a spokesman, told the New York Times: *'We don't consider ourselves sea bandits. We consider sea bandits those who illegally fish in our seas and dump waste in our seas and carry weapons in our seas. We are simply patrolling our seas. Think of us like a coastguard.'*

Richard Phillips, the captain of an American cargo ship, was rescued on 12 April 2009 after spending four days as a captive of Somali pirates.

What about the workers?

When the Industrial Revolution began,

many people's working and living conditions changed dramatically. Some of the changes were positive. For the first time, ordinary families could afford to buy some of the products that the new factories manufactured – clothing, furniture, books and even luxuries such as sets of dinner plates.

At the same time a number of social problems developed alongside the new national prosperity. Working conditions in many of the factories were dangerous and unhealthy, and some of the worst-affected workers were young children who began their working lives at the age of ten.

Working life today

Most developed countries experienced these upheavals more than two centuries ago and they have since improved their working practices and conditions. Workers can join together to form trade unions and other organizations to press their employers for improvements. Children are no longer forced to go out to work. Unfortunately, workers in many developing countries have not benefited from these improvements.

Hearing about difficult or poor working conditions in Peru or India might alarm many people in better off countries, especially if the developed world could help to improve them. The difficulty today is that companies in the developed world are contributing to the problem of poor working conditions elsewhere.

International help

Opposite: a young boy in Bangladesh looks up from the metal-stamping machine where he works most days. Child labour is still a major problem in many countries.

Many people in developed countries are concerned about workers' lives in the places where their clothes, fruit, drinks or sports equipment began their long journey from producer to consumer. Harsh working conditions (often involving young children) coupled with low prices, can lead to workers at the beginning of this trading chain being caught in a poverty trap. The term 'banana republic' arose as a mocking term to describe the way in which countries can find themselves tied to a single crop or other export. If prices drop – or are kept down by powerful consumer countries – these producer countries have no alternative source of income.

Dozens of international organizations aim to improve conditions and trading terms for these producer countries. These groups are known collectively as non-governmental organizations (NGOs) because they are not part of any country's government. They cannot make or enforce laws, but this helps them to remain neutral so they are not tied to any political party or movement. Instead they work to raise living standards and to help people to find new opportunities at a local level.

Coffee Kids

Coffee Kids was founded in the US in 1988. It is a leading NGO which aims to improve the lives of people in coffee-producing countries. Its website home page spells out why it exists: 'coffee is the second most traded commodity in the world after petroleum [oil]'. It is not one of the largest NGOs working in this field, but it provides a link between those who produce coffee and those who drink it. The money it spends comes from coffee-lovers in the developed world – coffee shops, coffee importers and individual coffee-drinkers.

As its name suggests, Coffee Kids focuses on children growing up in coffee-producing countries. These children are often very poor, have little decent food, and poor education and health care. Coffee Kids gives coffee-growing communities 'a hand up, not a handout'. Like other NGOs, Coffee Kids recognizes that women play an important role in helping to break this cycle of poverty. Working with other NGOs or on its own, it helps village women find the money they need to set up and build small businesses. These firms – which include beauty salons, food stands, pharmacies and commercial farms – help other villagers find ways to build new lives. Once they become less dependent on the coffee buyers (because they can find other work), they can press for better pay and conditions.

Another way to improve conditions in the developing world – while still supporting international trade – is for consumers to demand change. Many people in better off countries choose to buy products that they know are produced in conditions that benefit the workers. For example, the Fairtrade symbol on products sold in Britain indicates that they meet a series of strict standards. Fairtrade organizers – and the people who buy their products – aim to reverse some of the injustices in the world of international trade.

Women from a village in Togo in Africa grind local crops using a mill they bought with NGO money. Such projects enable villagers to earn income in new ways.

YOUR MONEY'S WORTH

Making the rules work

The international community has begun addressing a wide range of problems tied to world trade. Many countries have laws and regulations which protect many groups — including women, children, the elderly, the sick

and the poor — against unfair working practices. Can you think of any other groups that need help in this area? Can you suggest better ways to enforce existing rules and regulations?

Trade and the environment

International trade has far reaching

effects, not just on those people involved with it. Today, many people believe that unless action is taken urgently, the whole planet will suffer harm which may be irreversible. Their concern is focused on the effects of global commerce on the environment.

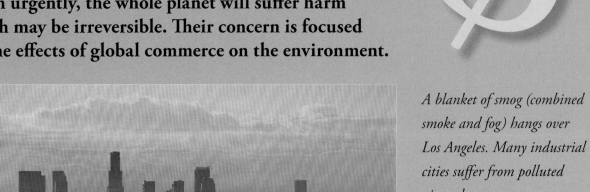

A blanket of smog (combined smoke and fog) hangs over Los Angeles. Many industrial cities suffer from polluted air and water.

As with many other issues, it is easier to explain this complicated problem by going back to basics. Imagine that someone buys a piece of land that is covered with valuable mature trees which can be used to make furniture. He immediately chops down a hundred trees, cuts them up for timber, and he sells them for a lot of money. Two years later he chops down another hundred trees and once more receives a good price for the wood they produce.

Measuring food miles

It is easy to understand how flooding valleys or chopping down rainforests to increase trade can harm the environment. But international trade can damage the environment in other ways.

One of those ways is through the effects of the extra carbon dioxide produced as a result of sending products long distances. This is particularly true of goods transported by air. Many products, such as fruit and flowers (which need to arrive fresh), are flown thousands of miles from their source to the countries where they are sold. Environmental activists describe these distances as food miles. They believe that the shorter the distance a product travels, the better – because there will be less damaging carbon released into the atmosphere.

A British website called the Organic Linker has a calculator on which people can work out the number of food miles some of their purchases have travelled. Visitors to the website can enter their own (destination) country and then the country where a product originated. Adding the type of product gives the site organizers a fuller picture of what is being transported – and where. The calculator then works out the distance travelled and the amount of carbon produced to travel this distance by plane, car or train. So, someone in London might find that the Egyptian tangerines on their kitchen table had travelled 3510 km (2181 miles) to reach them. And if that distance was covered by plane, 214 kg of carbon dioxide would have been released into the atmosphere.

Personal account

LOSING RAINFOREST

Professor Tim Lenton, from the University of East Anglia, points out how two trade-related trends can combine to make environmental problems worse.

'Losing the Amazon would be a tragedy for the planet and biosphere. When I was at school we feared we'd end up chopping it down and lose it that way. But now it looks like climate change might deal a killer blow. Unless we can restrict the warming and seasonal changes we're already seeing in the tropics, the prospects for the Amazon aren't good.'

Ten or twenty years later – depending on how much land he bought – the owner runs out of trees to cut down. By then the richest soil has been washed away from the areas that were once covered with trees. The soil that is left is not rich enough to nourish another grove or plantation of trees. Eventually the rain washes away even the remaining thin layer of soil, leaving an unproductive wasteland.

Better choices

The owner could have avoided the problem if he had been less selfish and more patient. If he had replanted trees where the first batch had been chopped down and waited longer before cutting down the next batch (to allow the newly-planted trees to begin growing), he could have continued the cycle without creating patches of wasteland. This sort of business is called sustainable because it can be repeated over and over again without harming the environment.

Similar problems exist on a global scale, fed by the demand to increase trade and people's unwillingness to look beyond a quick profit. We now know how damaging uncontrolled trade can be to the environment. Vast areas of forest (which provide habitats for wildlife and also help to balance the gases in the Earth's atmosphere) are cut down every year. The wood may be burnt for fuel, traded as timber or simply wasted as the ground is used to raise cattle for beef which goes into fast food burgers.

Animals are also hunted to the point of extinction in the name of international trade. Many species of whales are threatened, as well as tigers, rhinoceroses and other animals which are killed to make folk medicines. International trading organizations (see pages 34-37) now make the environment an important feature of any new agreements.

YOUR MONEY'S WORTH

Making a choice?

Imagine you have worked out the number of food miles (see Closer examination page 31) that some South African oranges have travelled to reach your kitchen. Now consider the living conditions in the village where those oranges were grown.

What would happen if you and other people in developed countries stopped buying those oranges and bought from producers closer to home? Would the benefits to the environment outweigh the hardship that it might bring to South African farmers?

Action and agreements

The world is a richer place because of international trade. People's lives have become more varied because they can use the whole world as a supermarket – trying out Indian scarves, Egyptian spices, Polish wooden toys or Canadian maple syrup. But this richness extends far beyond satisfying people's need for the new or imported goods. As a whole, the world is a richer place – in terms of money and income – because of global trade. Millions of people depend on it for their jobs and their future.

Opposite: NGO director-general Pascal Lamy (second from left) addresses a conference in Paris in January 2009. The conference discussed ways of combining social justice with international trade.

Ensuring that this trade operates in a fair and safe way is essential to ensure that this richness is maintained – and extended further to those who have yet to benefit from it. This requires the support and cooperation of many nations. Just as a single trader would go out of business if he constantly overcharged customers or otherwise offended them, so countries must find a balance between helping their own people and supporting a system that protects their traders, those in other countries and the planet itself.

Enlightened self-interest

Very few people – and even fewer countries – want to give away their wealth just because others are worse off. Most governments would be voted out of office if they decided that poorer countries should have massive discounts on what they buy. Instead, voters and governments want to improve their own interests in global trade (their self-interest).

Sometimes, this national advantage, or self-interest, is best served by helping the world's poorest countries through favourable trading deals. India, for example, is a good trading partner if it exports tea and cloth goods to Italy. It becomes a better partner for the Italians, though, if it becomes wealthy enough to buy Italian shoes, cars and refrigerators in return. Seen in those terms Italy, like other developed countries, might agree to trading measures which help the world's second-largest country. And India would naturally like to see its own people and companies become wealthier. In both cases, enlightened self-interest is an important motive in supporting trading agreements.

Ways forward

A number of international groups help to support and promote international trade. The most far-reaching is the World Trade Organization, which deals with 'the global rules of trade between nations'. It believes that breaking down barriers to world trade

The role of the media

Newspapers and broadcasting media help people understand some of the complicated issues surrounding international trade. They also draw attention to problems and injustices in the world economic system, wherever they may be. In October 2007, for example, the BBC publicized a report on child labour published in the *Observer* newspaper.

The *Observer* had photographed a ten-year-old boy working in an Indian clothing factory. The clothes were sold in Gap shops in Europe and North America. Interviewed by the newspaper, the boy said that he had been sold to a factory owner by his family, and that he had worked for four months without pay. He would not be allowed to leave the factory until the fee

that had been paid to his family was repaid. Dan Henkle, a spokesman for Gap, referred to the *Observer* and BBC reports: 'We were made aware earlier this week that a reporter had found an incident of children working in a factory that was producing for one of our brands, and this is completely unacceptable to us. We have a strict prohibition on child labour, and we are taking this very seriously. This is very upsetting and we intend to investigate thoroughly.'

The company withdrew the item produced by the Indian factory – a blouse – from its 3000 shops. It also set in motion an emergency examination of working conditions in all the factories that supply clothing.

The American trade union Unite has helped to publicize the poor working conditions that many people face in sweatshops around the world.

reduces similar barriers between nations. The World Trade Organization's 153 member countries account for 97 per cent of world trade.

Similar trading organizations or agreements cover specific regions. The European Union (EU) works for the interests of its 27 member-states – and their relationship with the rest of the world. The North American Free Trade Agreement (NAFTA) covers the United States, Canada and Mexico. Other organizations link countries with similar products – such as the Organization of Petroleum-Exporting Countries (OPEC) – to find the best trading strategies for their members.

YOUR MONEY'S WORTH

For or against the EU?

The origins of the European Union go back nearly 60 years, when six nations agreed to use policies and trades to 'make war not only unthinkable but materially impossible'. The memory of the Second World War was still fresh and painful. Since then, the union has grown to include 27 member states,

but its core aim – using trade as a tool to promote peace – remains important. Do you think that Europe is more peaceful and prosperous because of the European Union? Or do you agree with Eurosceptics, who believe the EU has removed many freedoms?

The bottom line

Money lies at the heart of international trade. Money itself is one of the main elements that is traded between countries. So it is not surprising that most international trading measurements are based on money. Economists and voters use these measurements to see how successfully a country is performing on the world stage.

The remote settlement of Glenorchy in New Zealand has seen a massive increase in foreign visitors since it was used as a setting for the Lord of the Rings *films.*

One of the most important measures is a country's balance of trade, which looks at the difference between the country's exports and imports over a period such as a month or year. It might seem that

Personal account

MIDDLE EARTH DOWN UNDER

'You could argue that Lord of the Rings was the best unpaid advertisement that New Zealand has ever had,' said Bruce Lahood, who promotes New Zealand tourism in North America.

'In the past decade, New Zealand has been the most successful country to benefit from movie tourism. We've been looked at and case-studied from many angles.'

The number of tourists visiting New Zealand has increased enormously. Its remote location, with only Australia as a near neighbour, has always limited the numbers of foreign visitors. But between 2000 and 2007, the number of foreign visitors to New Zealand jumped by 40 per cent – from 1.7 million to 2.4 million. Much of this increase was because of the popularity of the three Lord of the Rings films, which were filmed in New Zealand.

a positive balance (when more goods are exported than imported) is best, but some economists argue that if more money goes to other countries it might find its way back to the original country through other purchases. Overall trade might also be affected by changing exchange rates, which can make a country's products more or less expensive depending on which way the rates move. Perhaps the best measure of national wealth is to work out the gross domestic product and then divide this by the number of people living in the country.

Always changing

If there were one fail-safe way of calculating the value of trade, every country would adopt it. Unfortunately, it is very difficult to pin down exactly how – or where – people are spending their money in an age of instant international transactions. The nature of the world economy, and how people trade within it, is constantly changing. Some trends only become apparent once they have been happening for some time.

For example, as people around the world have become wealthier compared with their parents and grandparents, they are able to spend more on services. Tourism has an important place in international trade: some experts estimate that it earns £1.2 trillion (or £1,200,000,000,000) worldwide each year. This figure includes all spending by foreign visitors – on travel, food, accommodation, souvenirs and so on. So it is not surprising that countries work hard at attracting more tourists.

The ability to predict such trends can make a country's trade position stronger. That's another example of how the global economy reflects national or even individual experiences: being ahead of a trend is usually a key ingredient in business success.

Voices of protest

Individuals and groups have protested about the worst effects of international trade for years. Most of the protests single out an aspect of world trade, such as the human cost (see pages 26-29) or its destructive effects on the environment (see pages 30-33). The protesters are not necessarily trying to stop international trade – they simply want it to operate in a way that considers their particular cause.

Some protests, though, are aimed at the very heart of international trade, and especially at what we call globalization. Anti-globalization protesters argue that the current world economic system encourages huge companies to spread across the globe. This international approach does not, in their view, lead to greater trading exchanges between countries or societies. Instead it allows a dominant company to use its economic power to crush competitors in every country where it operates. Having eliminated most of the competition, the giant company can then force local workers and suppliers to accept poor deals. The largest anti-globalization protests often coincide with high-level meetings of world economic or trading organizations. Protesters disrupted the Seattle meeting of the World Trade Organization in December 1999, which led to 600 people being arrested. Less than two years later, anti-globalization groups converged on the Italian city of Genoa, where leaders of the G8 were meeting. The Genoa clashes were particularly violent, and one young protester was killed in a violent clash with police.

By early 2009, the G8 (the number stands for the number of countries involved) had grown to become the G20 and the world was struggling to deal with the effects of the credit crunch. Environmentalists joined anti-globalists in launching protests at the G20 meeting in London in March 2009. The latest protests also targeted banks, which many people believe contributed to – or even triggered – the world economic problems that began in 2007.

Opposite: a protester calling for fairer world trade stands outside a police ring at the G20 meeting in London in April 2009. Protests have become common at such international meetings.

Looking ahead

Throughout history there have been enormous changes in the way business is conducted around the world. Countries that continued to make outdated products (or to used outdated ways of selling them) lost out to those which adapted to new trends. Each transition – such as the dawn of railways, the replacement of sailing ships, computer trading and the advent of the Internet – has provided a boost to trade, but has left some countries unable to compete.

Some experts say that the only constant in the world is change itself. That can apply to international trade as much as to any human activity, but it is particularly important. Some turbulent events have slowed the growth of international trade – the World Trade Organization estimated that world trade declined by nine per cent in 2009 because of the credit crunch – but the underlying trend is for growth

UK prime minister Gordon Brown and US president Barack Obama pose with their wives in London before the G20 meeting in April 2009. Friendly relations between world leaders can help to smooth the way towards better international trade deals.

in trade. Nonetheless, it seems likely that this growth may go in some unexpected or little-known directions.

Newer and quicker

Growing international awareness of wider trade issues has led to new forms of international business. Some of the new areas of business – such as ecotourism and organic foods – have been hit hard during the credit crunch. People are less prepared to spend extra on these goods and services when the future of their own income may be shaky. But these areas of business are here to stay, and people who use them will help spread the word about the principles and causes that they represent.

Other areas of international trade will reflect the pace of change in the modern world. Already it is possible for someone sitting at a computer in New Zealand to buy land in Spain, sell a coin collection to a buyer in Argentina, view the latest American film and book a room in a remote hotel in Scotland. None of this would have been possible 20 years ago. The trade winners in the twenty-first century will be those countries, companies and individuals who can link their trade with the Internet and other forms of instant communication.

Personal account

WANTED:
GLOBAL SOLUTIONS

The British prime minister Gordon Brown welcomed newly-elected US president Barack Obama to London the day before the G20 leaders met in April 2009 to discuss the challenges of the global economic crisis.

'This is an unprecedented economic crisis. People have lost their homes, their jobs and in some cases their hope. And President Obama and I are agreed today that the actions we take are global solutions to global problems.'

Glossary

9/11   A series of violent terrorist attacks on the United States on 11 September (written 9/11 by Americans) 2001.

al Qaeda   An Islamic terrorist group with supporters in many countries.

balance of trade   The amount of money earned by a country's exports minus the amount spend on imports.

biosphere   The part of our planet in which life can exist.

capitalism   An economic system in which companies are run by private owners for profit, rather than owned by the state.

civilization   A society with well-developed arts, language and government.

commodity   A natural product that can be traded on its own (for example tea) or as a raw material (such as copper or iron).

communism   A political system in which property is owned by the community and people contribute and receive according to ability and need. The government provides work, health care, education and housing, but may deny people certain freedoms.

consumer   Someone who consumes (buys and uses) something.

credit   A banking term to describe lending and how easy it is to arrange it.

credit crunch   A period beginning in 2007 during which credit and other economic measures were severely affected.

developed countries   Countries with a long history of industrial production, usually among the wealthiest in the world.

developing countries   Countries with little or no history of industrial production, often among the poorest in the world.

economist   Someone who studies how the economy operates.

Eurosceptic   Someone who believes the European Union should have fewer powers and who wants those powers to be controlled by his or her country's government.

exchange rate   The amount of money in another currency that a unit of a national currency can buy at a given time.

export   To sell abroad, or goods sold abroad.

extinction   No longer surviving on Earth.

globalization   The spread of similar businesses and trading practices around the world.

gross domestic product   The total goods and services produced by a country.

import   To buy from abroad, or goods bought from abroad.

Industrial Revolution   The period during the 1700s and 1800s when manufacturing techniques changed the way people worked and the way goods were produced.

infrastructure   The roads, railway lines, canals and forms of communication that help trade in a country.

non-governmental organization (NGO)   An international organization run by people who are not linked to any government.

ration   To limit the amount of something that a person can buy because of shortages.

raw material   A basic ingredient (eg wood or minerals) used to make something else.

service   Activities that are paid for, and which do not transfer ownership of any object: tourism and travel are both services.

Silk Route   A network of overland routes connecting Asia with the lands around the Mediterranean Sea, including southern Europe and North Africa.

subsidies (singular: subsidy)   Money paid by governments to farms and other industries to help them compete with their foreign counterparts.

sustainable   Able to be repeated many times.

Taliban   An Islamic group which has struggled to gain (and then regain) control of Afghanistan.

transnational   A company that has branches in many countries.

Further reading

Free Trade Kathiann M. Kowalski (Marshall Cavendish Children's Books, 2007)

Globalize It!: The Stories of the IMF, the World Bank, the WTO, and Those Who Protest Brendan January (Twenty-First Century Books, 2007)

What Is Trade? Carolyn Andrews (Crabtree, 2008)

Websites

Coffee Kids
http://www.coffeekids.org/

Food Miles
http://www.organiclinker.com/food-miles.cfm

World Trade Organization (WTO)
http://www.wto.org/

Index